THE ARMENIANS IN AMERICA

THE **ARMENIANS** IN AMERICA

ARRA S. AVAKIAN

11150   Published by
Lerner Publications Company
Minneapolis, Minnesota

ACKNOWLEDGMENTS

The illustrations are reproduced through the courtesy of: pp. 6, 10, 12, 15, 20, 69, 82, Sovfoto; p. 13, British Museum; p. 18, Walters Art Gallery, Baltimore; p. 19, Bibliotheque Nationale, Paris; pp. 23, 43, 45, United Press International; p. 24, Armine Barseghian Thomason, Weston, Massachusetts, and Ruth Thomason, New York City, New York; pp. 27, 29, 30, 33, 41, 44, Haroutune P. Hazarian, New York City, New York, and Ruth Thomason; p. 32, Professor Nina Garsoian, Dean of Students, Princeton University, New Jersey, Jacques Kayaloff, New York City, New York, and Ruth Thomason; pp. 51, 61 (right), Fresno City and County Historical Society Archives; p. 53 (top), Whitney Museum of American Art; p. 53 (bottom), Hermine Der Harootian; p. 54, Macmillan Publishing Company, Incorporated; p. 55, Omar Khayyam's Restaurant; p. 56 (left), La Verne College; p. 56 (right), Bentley College; p. 57 (left), Masco Corporation; p. 57 (right), Sarkes Tarzian, Incorporated; p. 58, Peter Paul, Incorporated; p. 59, Charles Garry; p. 61 (left), Jill Krementz, Farrar, Straus and Giroux; p. 62, University of Minnesota Hospitals; p. 63, Minnesota Orchestra; p. 64, Metropolitan Opera Archives; p. 66, Bruce Harlan, University of Notre Dame; p. 67 (left), Rouben Mamoulian; p. 67 (right), Hanson and Schwam, Los Angeles, California; p. 72, Manoog Kaprielian, Armenian Youth Federation; p. 76, Takahashi Studio, Fresno, California; p. 79, Armenian General Benevolent Union Alex Manoogian School.

LIBRARY OF CONGRESS CATALOGING IN PUBLICATION DATA

Avakian, Arra S.
  The Armenians in America.

  (The In America Series)
  Includes index.
  SUMMARY: Discusses the history of the Armenian people and the numerous contributions made by Armenian immigrants and their descendants to the history and culture of the United States.

  1. Armenian American—Juvenile literature. 2. Armenians—History—Juvenile literature. [1. Armenian Americans. 2. Armenians—History] I. Title.

E184.A7A83   930'.004'91992   77-73739
ISBN 0-8225-0228-3 [Library]
ISBN 0-8225-1026-X [Paper]

International Standard Book Number: 0-8225-0228-3 Library Edition
International Standard Book Number: 0-8225-1026-X Paper Edition

Library of Congress Catalog Card Number: 77-73739

. . . CONTENTS . . .

The 13th-century monastery of Geghard, in Soviet Armenia, is one of the monuments from the Armenian past.

6

INTRODUCTION

The Armenian people have had their own distinctive language and culture for nearly 3,000 years. Today there are approximately 5,000,000 Armenians, about half of whom live in a small, rocky, mountainous land in southwestern Asia. This is all that is left of their ancient homeland in the Middle East. The rest of the Armenians are scattered in nearly every country of the earth. There are at least 25 separate nations where more than 10,000 Armenians have settled permanently.

The Armenian homeland is located just north of the Tigris-Euphrates Valley (the land of important ancient kingdoms such as Babylon and Assyria). In ancient times, it sat astride the great trade routes between Europe and the Mediterranean countries to the west and India and the Orient to the east. Because of its strategic position, Armenia has been sought as a prize by powerful nations throughout its long history. It was frequently under foreign domination, and its people were often forced to flee to escape

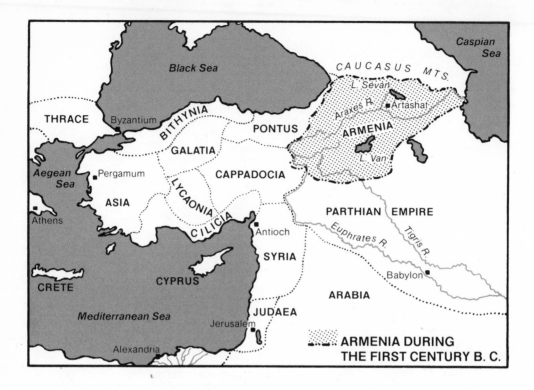

persecution. But the greatest dispersion occurred during the last decade of the 19th century and the early years of this century, when the wholesale slaughtering of Armenians by the Turks caused many thousands to flee for their lives. The climax came when virtually the entire remaining population of Armenians was forced by the Turkish government to leave the homeland. They were driven from their homes and from their land, their goods were taken, and they were either massacred or left to starve in the Syrian Desert. It was the first case of genocide in the 20th century, taking place long before Hitler tried to practice this kind of racial extermination on the Jews of Europe.

The United States has its share of the world's Armenians, although no one knows exactly how many there are. There may be about 500,000 now living in the country. This is nearly 10 percent of all Armenians, more perhaps than in any other country outside the homeland. The Armenians came to America in search of freedom, and they found their new country to be hospitable. Because they came without any material resources and without knowing the English language, it was difficult for them to establish themselves. But they had courage, they were self-reliant, and they were too proud to depend on charity from others. The immigrants were also industrious, possessing skills in the crafts and trades, and they were determined to succeed. As a result, they eagerly sought education. They worked hard, improved their skills, and learned the ways of the people of America. In two generations, they prospered, becoming merchants, artisans, doctors, lawyers, teachers, scientists, engineers, and industrialists.

The Armenians in America are now well-established in their chosen fields. They may be found everywhere in this country, but they are especially concentrated in New England and the Atlantic states, in the cities of Detroit and Chicago, and in Central and Southern California. The following pages tell the story of how this all came about.

These modern Armenians celebrating a wedding are the descendants of the people who settled in Armenia more than 3,000 years ago.

10

PART I

Who Are the Armenians?

1. *Origins*

Armenia is in the southwestern part of Asia, in that region just east of Greece and north of the Holy Land known as "Asia Minor." It lies in the highlands around Lake Van and Lake Sevan, where the Tigris and the Euphrates rivers begin their long course to the Persian Gulf, and where the Araxes River winds its ancient path to the Caspian Sea. This is where Mount Ararat (the place where Noah's Ark is supposed to have landed after the flood) stands prominently with its summit eternally covered with snow. The people who were living in this area around 1000 B.C. were known as "the people of Urartu," and it is from them that the name "Ararat" arises.

In about 800 B.C., a branch of the migrating Aryan people from the northwest moved into the same area. The mixture of the original inhabitants and the Aryan invaders formed the Armenian people we know today. The resulting population combined the strong physical characteristics of the native Urartians (a society of hardy mountain people, accustomed to the rigors of the severe climate) with the high cultural achievements of the newcomers.

The Armenians have a legendary account of their origins as well, and it explains why they call themselves "Hai," and their country "Haiastan." The earliest Armenian historian, Movses of Khoren, described the history of Armenians in the same allegorical way that the Bible describes the early history of humanity. According to Movses, a great-grandson of Noah by the name of Haik fought his cousin Bel for the right to live freely. He defeated Bel and started a nation named "Hai," after him. Scholars believe today that the story should really be the other way around. Movses of Khoren probably invented the hero called "Haik." The name "Hai" is, in fact, taken from the name of a small tribe of people who were living in the area.

Mount Ararat

2. Religion

In pagan times, before the rise of Christianity, Armenians worshipped a whole family of gods who resembled the ancient gods of the Greeks and Romans. Their chief god, Aramazd, corresponds to the Greeks' Zeus and the Romans' Jupiter. Astghik, the goddess of love and beauty, corresponds to Aphrodite (Greek) and Venus (Roman), and so on. The pagan Armenians were also animists: they believed that all natural objects had personalities and experienced human-like thoughts and feelings. If a person were to strike a tree, for example, he or she would have to ask its forgiveness.

A bronze head of the goddess Anahit, patron and protector of ancient Armenia

The Christian religion was brought to Armenia very soon after its establishment. According to tradition, the apostles Thaddeus and Bartholomew traveled in the regions of Armenia and spread the gospel of Christianity. The religion found ready acceptance among the common people, but the apostles encountered severe opposition from those who felt that their positions were endangered. Thus, it was not surprising that Thaddeus and Bartholomew suffered martyrdom in Armenia. Two ancient churches named after the two apostles still stand today near the traditionally accepted sites of their graves.

During the first 250 years of its history, Christianity in Armenia was practiced in secret, because Christians there, as elsewhere, were persecuted by the rulers of the day. But, toward the end of the third century, the Armenian king Tiridates decided not to persecute the Christians but rather to support them and even to become one himself. He converted to Christianity and became a devout believer, largely through the efforts of Gregory, his court secretary, who had long been a Christian. Today, the Armenians consider Gregory to be their patron saint; the members of the Armenians' Christian church are sometimes called "Gregorians," after St. Gregory.

Under the personal direction of Tiridates, Armenians throughout the land were converted to Christianity. Old pagan temples were destroyed, and Christian churches were built. This activity began in Armenia in the closing years of the third century, but it was not until the early part of the fourth century that Christianity became an accepted religion throughout the large and powerful Roman Empire. For this reason, Armenia is said to be the first Christian nation in the world.

In 451 A.D., Armenia became involved in a life-and-death struggle with its powerful neighbor, Persia. The Persian king was so dedicated to his own religion, called "Zoroastrianism," that he wanted the Armenians to give up Christianity and embrace his faith. When the Armenians refused to comply with his wishes, the Persian king attacked. The Armenian army went into battle against the much larger Persian army, and they put up such a fierce resistance that the Persian king decided to abandon his effort to convert the Armenians to Zoroastrianism. It is because of this famous battle that the Armenians can claim to be the first nation to go to war to defend the Christian faith.

An Armenian church on the shore of Lake Sevan. Built during the ninth century, it makes use of the distinctive Armenian style of church architecture.

In the early days of Christianity, all Christians belonged to one universal church. There were no separate denominations, and representatives from many countries participated in world-wide meetings of Christian bishops, called "ecumenical councils." The first of these councils was held in the year 325 A.D. At the fourth ecumenical council, held in 451 A.D., the bishops debated a difficult issue of church doctrine concerning the nature of Christ. The Armenians did not accept the decision of the council, and they decided to remain apart from the main body of Christians. As a result, they formed an independent national church, with its own spiritual head, a church that still exists today.

When the Armenian national church was established, the people of Armenia wanted to build new church buildings in a style that was unique and that expressed the Christian faith as the Armenians felt it. For this reason, a new style of church architecture was developed. Constructed completely of stone, solid and massive, the new churches gave the worshippers a feeling of spaciousness. A central dome rising high overhead gave the whole structure a lofty appearance. The churches built on this plan, many of which are more than 1,000 years old, still stand today, in spite of centuries of exposure to the severe climate, to frequent earthquakes, and to military attacks. Armenian churches built in the United States still follow the architectural features of the early churches.

The Armenian Church survives today little changed from the time when it first became an independent national church. The religious rituals are still full of ceremony and color, the participants wear intricate and beautiful vestments, and nearly all of the observances are still sung or chanted. The highest form of the worship is the celebration of the Divine Liturgy, the "Holy Mass" of the western catholic churches.

3. Language

The language spoken by the early Armenians was brought in by the Aryan invaders who migrated to the region of Armenia in 800 B.C. At that time, however, the Armenian language was most likely not a written language. When Christianity became widespread throughout Armenia and the people worshipped in their new churches, it became necessary to use materials written either in Greek or in Assyrian. But the ordinary village priests and the worshippers themselves did not know either Greek or Assyrian. This situation held back the development of the church for 100 years. Finally, at the beginning of the fifth century A.D., the religious patriarch Sahak and the scholar Mesrop fashioned a new alphabet containing 36 letters, which could be used to write the Armenian language. This same alphabet (with two additional letters added) is still used by Armenians everywhere.

After Mesrop had completed his work of establishing an Armenian alphabet, the Bible was translated into Armenian. This translation was of such high quality that an early scholar called it the "Queen of Translations." Soon, other important works known to the civilized world were translated into Armenian, and new books were written by a large number of dedicated scholars, who made the Armenian literary tradition long, rich, and varied.

Many of these works written in Armenian are rare examples of the ancient art of bookmaking. Printing on printing presses was not invented until the 15th century, and the books that were produced before this time were carefully written by hand, on parchment. (Paper was not used until several hundred years later.) Very important books were illustrated with hand-drawn colored pictures and were decorated with colorful and beautiful border designs. For this reason, these old books are usually called "illuminated manuscripts." Enemy armies have invaded Armenia many times, and they have sacked and burned the churches, monasteries, and other places where national treasures, including old manuscripts, were kept. Over the years, tens of thousands of manuscript volumes have been destroyed or stolen, yet today there still exist at least 25,000 volumes of old Armenian manuscripts. Today, they are kept in special libraries, in museums, and in a few private collections. This immense number of illuminated manuscripts shows how much the early Armenians loved education and learning.

The language of the early writings is the classical, or written, tongue. In Armenian it is called *grabar*, which means "written." But the spoken language has changed greatly over the centuries, and it is now quite different from classical Armenian. This spoken language is called *ashkharabar*, and it is the every-day speech of modern Armenians throughout the world. *Grabar*, or classical Armenian, is still used in church services and is still studied by educated Armenians. The Armenian language is pleasant to hear. All the letters in each word are pronounced fully—none is slurred or pronounced unstressed. Classical scholars believe that the

A page from an Armenian illuminated manuscript, written and illustrated during the 13th century meaning of words and the grammar of classical Armenian are the same today as they were in the fifth century, when the language matured. This fact is important for two reasons. Scholars who are interested in the Scriptures find it helpful to refer to the old Armenian texts of the Bible to shed light on the meaning of passages that are sometimes obscure. In addition, linguists who study the interrelationship of languages find that Armenian is a helpful bridge that ties together a number of linguistic subjects. Armenian root words, for example, sometimes appear to be the source of words used in other languages of ancient times.

A coin from the first century B.C. bearing the image of Tigranes II

4. *Political History*

After its beginnings in 700 B.C., the Armenian nation grew steadily. It extended its influence over an increasingly larger geographical area, so that by 100 B.C., Armenia extended from the shores of the Caspian Sea in the east to the Mediterranean Sea in the west. This high point in Armenia's political and military power was achieved under the reign of Tigranes II, known as "Tigranes the Great." But Armenia's very success was, in a sense, the cause of its downfall. Rome, Armenia's powerful neighbor to the west, would not allow another nation to grow strong enough to challenge its own power. Rome marshalled its military strength and eventually reduced Armenia to its original geographical boundaries. By the time of Christ, Armenia was once again a small and self-contained nation. The period under Tigranes the Great was the highest point in Armenia's political history. No other Armenian ruler ever succeeded in surpassing the gains he had made.

The ruined walls of a fortress at Artashat, the capital of ancient Armenia. Behind the fortress stands a monastery built many centuries later.

After its conflict with the Romans, Armenia grew stronger again. During the first five centuries A.D., the country embraced Christianity, adopted a national alphabet, and made the great literary and religious achievements that we have already described. During the period from the fifth to the ninth centuries, however, the country became divided into many small regions called "principalities," ruled by individual princes who maintained their own armies. The people of the region tilled the soil, carried on trade and commerce, and served in the army. During this feudal period, Armenian lands were constantly exposed to attack. In the seventh century, for example, the Arabs conducted raids to gain tribute and invasions to acquire land.

In the 11th century, a major invasion took place. Seljuk Turks from the East invaded Armenia and overthrew the ruling families, many of whom fled to the west, taking large bands of followers with them. These people then settled near the shores of the Mediterranean, on the southern slopes of the Taurus Mountains. Many Armenians were already living there, descendants of the people who had gone to the area during the time of Tigranes, centuries earlier. This new region occupied by Armenians was known as Cilicia, and it survived as an independent nation for 300 years. The fall of Cilician Armenia came as a result of further Turkish invasions that reached their climax with the capture of Constantinople by the Turks in 1453. After this time, all Asia Minor came under the rule of the Ottoman Turks. The last Armenian king was Leon V, who died in 1393.

The period from 1400 to 1700 was a dark age for all Armenians in Asia Minor. During this time, the Armenians had no government of their own, no schools, and no freedom. They lived as a subject people under the absolute rule of the Turkish sultans. They were Christians in a Moslem world, and they could not enjoy the normal rights of citizens. The Armenians lived in Armenia, but Armenia did not belong to them.

In the 18th century, Armenian intellectuals living in foreign countries learned of the nationalistic spirit that was awakening in Europe. They saw other peoples seek and find national independence, sometimes at the cost of much bloodshed. These Armenian intellectuals felt that their own people should rise and fight for their freedom and independence. Soon they began to express their ideas in writing. They wrote poems, essays, novels, and articles; they published journals and smuggled them into Turkey to be distributed to the Armenians there.

Gradually, the Armenians in Turkey began to demand the rights and privileges that had been denied them. By the second half of the 19th century, this protest movement had attracted so much attention that Europe grew concerned about the terrible persecution that Armenians were suffering at the hands of the Turkish sultans. In 1877, Russia and the European powers demanded that the Turkish government make important reforms in its treatment of Christians within the Empire. The sultans did not carry out these reforms, however, and the persecutions against the Armenians were redoubled. All of Europe began to talk about "the Armenian Question," but none of the European powers took action to help the Armenians. The persecutions continued. In Turkey, revolutionary groups of Armenians began to form, dedicated to ending the Turkish oppression and gaining normal human rights for the Armenians. Many Armenians emigrated to Europe, to America, to Russia, and elsewhere during this troubled time.

In 1914, World War I broke out, and emigration of Armenians out of Turkey was virtually halted. It was then that the darkest period in all of Armenian history took place. The Turkish government had sided with the Central Powers in the War. On the pretext that the Armenians were supporting the Allies (Turkey's enemies), the Turkish government decided to massacre them. Two million Armenians were driven from their homes and forced to march into the Syrian desert. In the process, one and one-half

Refugees fleeing the massacres in Armenia during the early years of the 20th century

million Armenians died or were slain. This was half of all the Armenians living under Turkish rule. When the massacre had ended, only a few tens of thousands remained in the interior. Some had also managed to escape to the Russian provinces where Armenians lived.

The Armenians in Constantinople (about 150,000) were relatively unhurt: Constantinople was a cosmopolitan city, and there were many foreigners living there. No wholesale massacre would go unnoticed. But the leaders of the Armenian community, many of whom lived in Constantinople, were all arrested on April 24, 1915, and either imprisoned or killed outright. This left the Armenians without leaders who could organize resistance to the Turks' plan of mass slaughter. In honor of these slain leaders, Armenians all over the world still commemorate April 24 as Armenian Martyrs' Day.

All the members of this Armenian family except the child on the left were killed during the Turkish massacres.

The early years of World War I brought unrelieved tragedy to the Armenians in Turkey, but the Armenians who lived in Russia were more fortunate. In 1917, the Tsarist government of Russia was overthrown, and that part of the old Armenian homeland that had been under Russian rule was left by itself. In 1918, the Armenians of the region set up an independent republic. The new government issued currency and postage stamps, and it established diplomatic relations with a number of countries, including the United States. But the independent republic did not last long.

Even after the general armistice that supposedly ended the war in 1918, fighting continued in the east. In 1920, both Turkish and Russian forces attacked Armenia. Before long, the young republic fell, and its land was divided between the Soviet Union and Turkey.

That part of Armenia which remained in Soviet hands became a soviet republic, and it is now part of the modern Soviet Union. With a population of about 2,500,000, the Armenian Soviet Socialist Republic remains as the only surviving Armenian state, but it contains only about one-tenth of the original Armenian homeland. The rest, which is now part of central Turkey, has only about 20,000 Armenians still living in it.

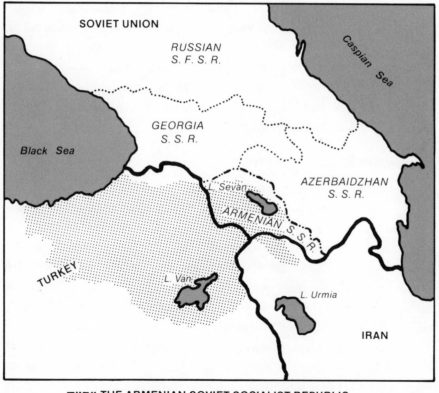

— · — · — THE ARMENIAN SOVIET SOCIALIST REPUBLIC
░░░░ THE INDEPENDENT REPUBLIC OF ARMENIA (1918)

5. Culture and Society

When the Armenian immigrants first arrived in America, they brought with them a set of customs and traditions hundreds of years old. Many of these traditions were abandoned as soon as the Armenians reached the New World, while others have survived as part of the distinctive way of life of the Armenian-American community. Before we turn to the subject of how the Armenians came to America and made new lives here, we will first consider how they lived in the past in the old Armenian homeland.

Each people has its own characteristic culture, and the Armenians are no exception. Yet many parts of Armenian culture are related to the cultures of their neighbors. For example, their poetry is related to the poetry of Persia and other cultures of the Middle East. Their foods are similar to those of other people of the eastern Mediterranean region. Their traditional costumes are like those of other peoples in the mountainous highlands of Asia Minor. On the other hand, Armenian music and church architecture are distinctive and unique.

Family and Social Structure

In the agricultural provinces of the Armenian homeland, the family was strongly patriarchal. The eldest male of the family was the head of a large and diverse household, consisting of his wife, their sons, the brides that came into the family by marriage to the sons, the grandsons and their brides, and so on. Because each family would have many children, it was not unusual for a single household to consist of several dozen people who belonged to three or four different generations. This immense household, called an "extended family," lived under the nearly absolute control of the eldest male, or patriarch. The many different relationships between individuals produced numerous combinations of relatives, and there were more than a dozen specific

The members of a large Armenian family pose for a
wedding picture in 1901. The bride is only 15 years old.

names to identify each combination. There were terms for bride,
husband's father, husband's mother, husband's brother, husband's
sister, husband's brother's wife, sister's husband, father's brother,
father's sister, and so on.

In general, marriages were arranged by the parents of the
bride and groom. Sometimes there were matchmakers, or go-
betweens, who arranged marriages between the sons and the
daughters of different households. Because of this custom, of
arranged marriages, it was not at all uncommon for the bride and
groom to marry without ever having seen one another. Even during
the wedding ceremony itself, the groom could not see the face
of his bride, for she would be heavily veiled. In some regions, the
bride and groom were not even permitted to come together until
two or three days after the actual wedding ceremony, for until
then the wedding guests might still be gathered in merry-making.

The average age of a bride and groom was low by our standards: it was common for a boy of 17 to marry a girl of 15. But there was no economic or social challenge that such a newly married young couple had to face. They simply fitted into the existing extended-family household where the groom already lived.

The traditional marriages arranged by parents were permanent. Divorce was out of the question; it simply did not exist. Since marriages were most often arranged within the same village, hundreds of years of intermarriage meant that virtually everyone was related to everyone else, one way or another. But care was taken that the relationship was not too close. The church defined the degree of blood relationship that was permitted in a marriage.

Religious Life

In the old world, every aspect of life was closely connected with the church. All of the people in a small area within a village belonged to the same church parish, and the church's laws and traditions fitted together harmoniously with the daily living habits of the people. Attendance at church was important not only on Sunday; many people attended church daily, if only for a few minutes. Liturgical services took place several times a day, and the church was always open for the faithful to enter. The dietary habits of the people were regulated by the church laws, which were related to the climate of the area, the seasons, and the village way of life.

With its various feast days, days of abstinence, and special practices, the calendar of the church was, in effect, the calendar by which the people lived. It was common practice, for example, to name children according to the day designated in the church calendar at the time the child was born. A male child born on (or very near) the church date dedicated to St. Gregory would be named Gregory. A boy born at Easter time would be named Haroutiun, which is the Armenian word for the Resurrection.

A portrait of two Armenian priests (front) taken around 1912. The church and the clergy played an important role in Armenian life.

Education

Before the middle of the 19th century, there was very little opportunity for formal education in old Armenia because Armenian schools were generally not permitted to exist. After that time, there were some schools, but education in a formal sense was available only to a select few. The schools that did exist

The students at an Armenian boys' school in Caesarea, Turkey, 1898

were private, and they were owned and run by individuals who had been educated in one of the larger cities where there were schools for higher education. Such a person would often continue his education until his early twenties and then return to his native village to open a school. Or he might join with the schoolmaster of an already existing school. Families that were better off or that put a higher value on formal education would send their boys (usually not the girls) to such schools. The village schoolmaster was a highly respected person. He had strong disciplinary rights over the children in his school. Often, the schoolmaster was a writer as well, and he would write books, poetry, or articles for periodicals published in the cities.

Students who showed special aptitude for education would, if their families could afford it, be sent to the largest cities of Armenia, or even to Europe, to gain a full education. Each of the larger cities of old Armenia had a college. In more recent years, but before the dispersion, more and more young men (and also women) began to obtain a higher education.

Children who did not attend school at all obtained what might be called a "home education." They learned the basics of agriculture, trade and commerce, and various crafts from their parents and other family members. Along with developing their skills in these practical activities, the children were taught general facts. It should not be said that these children were uneducated, only that they did not obtain a formal education in regular schools. They learned what they needed to know, and they were well-prepared to form part of the culture and society in which they lived and in which they would mature.

Folk Customs

Although the Armenians shared their ancient homeland with other cultures and societies, they have remained a distinct people with their own folk customs. Some of these customs are left over from their old pagan religion. The rest are mostly part of the Christian way of life and are associated with the church and its calendar of feasts and events. A few of these ancient customs seem to have arisen independently of any religious tradition.

Perhaps the biggest nonreligious feast day in old Armenia was New Year's Day, when a jolly old man brought the children gifts. There was visiting with relatives, and there were many good things to eat. This was one of the happiest times of the year. Christmas itself was celebrated on January 6, and it was a purely religious holiday. The Armenian Church celebrates the birth of Jesus, his revelation to the Wise Men, and his baptism all together on this one day, which they call *Theophany*, meaning "revelation of God." Because the holiday period of New Year's and Christmas came during the winter, there were few household or agricultural tasks that the villagers had to perform. Thus, they had time to enjoy themselves.

In traditional Armenian life, there was very little formal entertainment, such as concerts, plays, or sporting events. Nor was there radio or other forms of entertainment that could come into the home from the outside. People found recreation in simple gatherings: they would sing, dance, play games, tell stories, and compare experiences. Often, when people gathered together for recreation, they also engaged in useful household tasks such as spinning, weaving, sewing, mending, embroidering, and preparing food. Such gatherings occurred often in village life. There would also be feast days according to the religious calendar; there would be special festivities for weddings and baptisms; and there would be spontaneous gatherings whenever people simply wanted to be together and have a good time.

An Armenian woman wearing an elaborate festival costume

Like this antique dealer from Caesarea, many Armenians in Turkey were successful merchants and businessmen.

6. *Economic Life*

Among the many different peoples living in Asia Minor, in the 19th century, there was a general agreement that the Armenians were leaders in commerce and trade. Other nationalities within the Turkish Empire were also engaged in these fields, but it was the Armenians who dominated.

In a country that has not developed industrially, it is characteristic for business to be done on an individual basis. Tradespeople own their own tiny shops, and they may have their children working with them to sell the wares and to learn the trade. But there are no large stores employing dozens of people. The craftsmen—tailors, shoemakers, jewellers, bakers, and smiths—all operate their own businesses. This is what life in Armenia was like before the industrial revolution. There were no factories, and even the schools were run as small, private institutions. For this reason, the Armenians who became scattered throughout the world before and after World War I carried with them not only the trades and crafts in which they were highly skilled, but also a detailed knowledge of all aspects of the business. We shall see later how that fact influenced their new lives in other countries, especially in America.

Although the trades and crafts were important in Armenia, the economy was primarily agricultural. The country's natural resources were fertile land and sunshine. There was little rainfall during the summer months, but in the winter there was much snow that, with the spring thaw, filled the mountain streams and provided good irrigation. The use of electric power and the development of modern irrigation systems came very late in Armenia's history. The only effective agriculture in traditional times was limited to the land near streams and in the narrow river valleys. Some land was irrigated with water pumped by hand, and some crops, such as winter wheat, could grow without irrigation. Besides wheat, the most important agricultural products were other grains, cotton, hay, grapes, fruits, nuts, and certain vegetables. Sheep were the most important kind of livestock. They provided the main source of meat in the Armenian diet, and wool was the main textile fiber. Like other people of the Middle East, the Armenians produced fine oriental rugs, each design characteristic of the region in which it was produced.

Another important resource of Armenia was its minerals: copper, tin, zinc, and iron. Copper was combined with zinc and tin to produce brass and bronze; these metals were used to make many of the everyday household items of traditional times. In fact, recent discoveries have shown that the world's first steel furnaces may have been built in ancient Armenia as long as 3,000 years ago.

From the very earliest times, Armenian merchants traveled to remote foreign countries to set up trading posts and carry on international trade. They organized caravans to cross the land, and they chartered ships to cross the seas. They traded not only by exporting what Armenia produced but also by importing the products Armenia needed. They also carried on trade among other countries, acting as middlemen, developing markets, and finding sources of products. Thus, from very early times, small communities of Armenians became established in many countries of the world. When it was necessary for large numbers of Armenians to leave their homes and take refuge abroad, the fact that there were already Armenians in faraway places made it easier for these migrations to take place.

7. *Population*

There are probably more than 5 million Armenians in the world today, but Armenians may not have been quite so numerous in the past. Until the 19th century, nearly all Armenians lived in the same general region of Asia Minor. The rest were to be found in Europe, Russia, Persia, India, and the eastern shores of the Mediterranean. During the period when the countries of Europe were concerned about the persecution of Armenians in Turkey, numerous studies were made to estimate the number of Armenians living in the various parts of the world. When the first studies were made, the distribution of Armenians was something like this:

Distribution of Armenians in 1885

Russia and the Russian provinces of Armenia	2,000,000
Turkey	2,700,000
Persia	140,000
India and the Far East	20,000
The Near East and Africa	48,000
Western Europe	20,000
Southern and Eastern Europe	70,000
North America	1,000
South America	(very few)
Other Regions	(very few)
Total	4,999,000

But after the massacres of 1895 and 1915, the distribution looked something like this:

Distribution of Armenians in 1920

Armenia (including Russia & Transcaucasia)	2,100,000
Turkey	250,000
Persia	140,000
India and the Far East	20,000
The Near East and Africa	300,000
Western Europe	20,000
Southern and Eastern Europe	70,000
North America	100,000
South America	(very few)
Other regions	(very few)
Total	3,000,000

The Second World War and the rise of modern society has also had its effect on the Armenian population. In recent years, the distribution has been estimated as follows:

Distribution of Armenians in 1976

The Soviet Union (including the Armenian Soviet Socialist Republic)	3,800,000
Turkey	100,000
Iran (formerly Persia)	200,000
India and the Far East	16,000
The Near East and Africa	400,000
Western Europe	200,000
Southern and Eastern Europe	33,000
North America	545,000
South America	120,000
Other regions	30,000
Total	5,444,000

Even now, these latest figures are changing again. For example, the governmental policies of some of the Mediterranean countries are causing difficulties for Armenians, and many are seeking new homes. They are leaving Turkey, Egypt, Lebanon, and Syria and are going to countries in the Western Hemisphere, especially to the United States and Canada. Many are also going to South America, principally to Brazil and Argentina. These migrating Armenians of modern times establish themselves quickly in their new home countries. They bring with them their strong and proud tradition of industriousness, self-reliance, and perseverance. Many have come with special skills in crafts, trades, or the professions. As immigrants, they have often had to overcome many social and even legal obstacles placed before them, but they have experience in competing in a difficult environment. The effect of these hardships has been that they have emerged strong and well able to cope with the demands of building a new life in a new land.

PART II

The Armenian Immigration to America

1. *The Earliest Arrivals (1620-1890)*

The American colonies were in their infancy when the first Armenians appeared in North America. A man named "Martin the Armenian" was a member of the British colony in Jamestown, Virginia, which was established in 1620. Not long after this, the early colonists in Virginia began to raise silkworms, which they hoped would become an important industry in the colony. But the venture did not do well; it needed the assistance of experts in the art. Two Armenians, specialists in silk culture and production, were brought from their native land to help. Their assistance was considered so important that the Assembly of Virginia decided to subsidize their work. In 1656, it voted to give 4,000 pounds of tobacco to a certain "George the Armenian" as a special inducement for him to stay in Virginia and continue his work.

Aside from such isolated individuals, there was no significant migration of Armenians to the United States until the early 19th century, when a resourceful young man named Khachik Oskanian immigrated in 1834. Oskanian was the first of a growing number of Armenians who would come to America during this period. Who was this young man, and why did he seek a new life in the United States? To answer these questions, we will have to take another look at the situation that existed in the Armenian homeland in that time.

As we have described earlier, the Armenians had lived for centuries as a Christian nation within the Moslem nation of the Ottoman Turks. In the Ottoman Empire, religious and civil laws were combined, and only Moslems could be full citizens of the country. Armenians, under the leadership of the Armenian Patriarch of Constantinople, were allowed to rule themselves with their own body of combined religious and civil laws. But these laws were subject to the absolute and overriding law of the Empire. The Armenian community was not allowed to provide its own schools or to establish other cultural institutions that would help to preserve its distinct ethnic identity. Thus, the lives of Armenians in Turkey were severely restricted in many ways.

In the early 19th century, events occurred that would eventually bring a change to the lives of some of these Armenians. During these years, Protestant missionaries from America came to Turkey to try and convert its Moslem inhabitants. But their efforts were in vain, for it is an unpardonable sin for Moslems to give up their faith. So the missionaries turned their energies toward the Armenians, who, of course, were already members of an ancient Christian church. The missionaries opened mission schools, which were attended by many young Armenians eager to gain an education by any means. Some Armenian students were converted to Protestantism, and after they completed their educations in the mission schools, a select few were sent to America for further study. Thus it was that Khachik Oskanian, the first of a series of young students, came to America in 1834.

Oskanian quickly adapted himself to his new life in the United States. He graduated from the College of the City of New York and entered the field of journalism, becoming a feature writer for the *New York Herald.* His stories about life in the Near East were popular with the readers of his day, and the American public was introduced to Armenians through his work. Oskanian called the Armenians the "Yankees of the Near East." He was a promoter as well as a journalist. Taking advantage of the Homesteading Laws of the United States, he tried to encourage other Armenians to emigrate from Turkey to America. He wanted to build a new city in Ohio and name it after the ancient Armenian capital city of Ani. He even had plans drawn of the city, but in the end this ambitious plan did not materialize. Nevertheless, Oskanian led a long and active life, and his home in New York became a kind of way station for many Armenian immigrants who followed him to America.

By 1854, about 20 Armenian immigrants had arrived in the United States, mostly due to the activities of the missionaries. Among this group was Kristapor Seropian, a veterinarian who was also interested in pharmacy. In his work, he developed a green dye that became important as an ingredient for printing inks. (It is said that this same dye is used today in the ink that prints United States currency.) Seropian sold his discovery for $6,000, a tidy sum in the 19th century. He then took up the study of medicine, eventually becoming a licensed physician.

The early immigrants like Oskanian and Seropian were a colorful and select group, successful in life despite being displaced to a new land that was very different from their own. But this was to be expected, for it took resourcefulness, self-confidence, and courage to leave the old country and to face the challenge of this new life.

By 1870, there were about 70 Armenians in America, living mostly in New York and also in Boston. Profitable work in the wire mills of Worcester, Massachusetts, attracted one Armenian who in turn brought others, planting the seed for a large community that would eventually form there. Soon, this process was occurring in other cities in the Northeast. As students, merchants, and professionals, the immigrants spread out through Massachusetts, New Jersey, and Pennsylvania. By 1890, the total number of Armenians in America had reached about 2,000. Until then,

These Armenian merchants in New York City were well established
in the fur-importing business by the early years of the 20th century.

the immigrants had all arrived as individuals, each one separately,
each one under a different set of circumstances. But after the
initial trickle (mostly generated by the missionaries), a few more
decided to try it too.

One ailing Armenian merchant, newly arrived in Worcester,
discovered that he needed a warmer, drier climate for his health.
He settled in Fresno, California, arriving there with his brother
in 1881. They very quickly found the climate and growing conditions ideal for the Armenian way of life, and they lost no time
in writing to their native city of Marsovan, urging their friends and
relatives to join them in Fresno. The attraction was so great that
in 1883 a group of 45 immigrants arrived together in Fresno,
eager to be where there were "boat-sized watermelons," "egg-
sized grapes," and "nine- or ten-pound eggplants."

2. *The Beginning of Mass Immigration (1890-1899)*

Conditions in the Old World at the end of the 19th century set the stage for the first large-scale movement of Armenian immigrants to America. The treatment of Armenians in Turkey had worsened, and simple persecution had turned into mass murder. The first massacres expanded into massive killings, first of tens of thousands, then of hundreds of thousands. In 1894 and 1895, more than 300,000 Armenians were massacred in Turkey, most of them in the interior provinces (where the Armenians were more numerous and where there were fewer foreigners to witness the killings). Life had become unbearable. The Armenians' property was seized, and Armenian women were forcibly taken into harems. The most able-bodied men were tortured and murdered.

Under these horrible circumstances, many Armenians searched desperately for a way to leave Turkey. But leaving was not easy. It was necessary to make contact with friends outside Turkey, to collect enough money to secure passage out of the country, and to arrange transportation for themselves and for the few personal goods they could take with them. The only available transportation out of the interior was by horse-drawn cart, over mountainous roads that were sometimes hardly more than crude trails. The refugees were harassed by local officials who usually demanded heavy bribes before allowing them to pass. But many succeeded in escaping in spite of these difficulties, and they made their way to the United States. At this time, America was the new land of opportunity. All Armenians in their homeland had heard of the great new democracy in the Western Hemisphere where people were free and where all had equal opportunities to work, to gain an education, and to prosper.

It would hardly have been possible for so many Armenians to choose America as their new land of opportunity without the

Armenian refugees fleeing from the Turks

aid of the tiny colony of students, professionals, and businessmen who had already established themselves there. And American immigration laws of that time, which allowed almost anyone in good health to enter and look for work, also encouraged the entry of large numbers of immigrants. Thus, in the last decade of the 19th century, about 20,000 Armenians came to America to build new lives far from their troubled homeland.

3. *The Second Wave of Immigrants (1900-1914)*

The flow of Armenians to America that began in the last decade of the 19th century continued during the first decade of the 20th century. It was then that the largest groups came: whole extended families, including young married couples, children, infants, cousins, aunts, uncles, and grandparents. Many of those who came as children at that time are still alive today. The newcomers made their homes in communities where Armenians were already

In the period before World War I, whole Armenian families emigrated to the United States. This family made their home in Troy, New York.

gathered, generally living very close together. At the center of most Armenian communities there was usually a church: the first of these was established in 1890, in Worcester, Massachusetts. Other churches followed soon after, and by 1914 there were about 30 church communities in all, counting both the Armenian churches and the Protestant churches. In 1898, the Armenian church in the United States became a separate diocese with its 30 church communities in all, counting both the Armenian churches and the Protestant churches. In 1898, the Armenian church in the United States became a separate diocese with its own bishop. Previously, the churches had been under the spiritual authority of the Armenian Patriarch of Constantinople.

When Turkey became involved in the Balkan Wars, the flow of immigration greatly diminished. Then, with the outbreak of World War I in 1914, it became virtually impossible for Armenians to leave Turkey or to secure passage across the Atlantic. But by this time, the number of Armenians in America had grown to about 100,000.

4. *The Third Wave of Immigrants (1915-1924)*

When World War I ended, the immigration of Armenians resumed in large numbers. Between 1914 and 1924, about 25,000 Armenian immigrants entered America. Then in 1924, new and more restrictive immigration laws became effective in the United States. These new restrictions set a limit, or "quota," on the number of people who would be allowed to immigrate into the country each year from each nation of the world. The number of people

A group of young Armenian refugees awaiting resettlement, 1920

allowed to immigrate from Turkey (not only Armenians but all residents of Turkey) was the pitifully small figure of 100 persons per year!

Few of the immigrants who arrived during the period between 1915 and the restriction of immigration in 1924 came as members of closely knit family groups. After the massacres, the forced marches and refugee camps, and the confusion caused by World War I, many large family groups were completely broken up. The bulk of those who found their way to America in this period consisted of single individuals, orphans, and chance groupings of people. To some extent, America became a meeting-place for the reunion of many groups and families whose members had lost track of each other. The disruption of Armenian society during this period was so complete and the people so widely scattered, that even today elderly people are still seeking (and sometimes finding) their long-lost relatives. In some cases, even brothers and sisters who were separated during the time of the massacres are now discovering each other again. The greatly improved international communication and travel of the modern world is making it possible for these miracles to unfold.

5. Recent Immigration

The end of World War II ushered in a new period of Armenian immigration to America. There were no longer many Armenians left in Turkey. But large numbers of them lived in countries overrun by the war, and many had lost their homes and families. A special provision for "displaced persons" allowed such people to enter the United States and become residents. Under this provision, a large number of Armenians came to the United States. These new immigrants came from southern and eastern Europe, where many had been displaced by the battling armies as they surged back and forth across Europe. They came from Egypt, where new national policies made it less hospitable for Armenians.

They came from Turkey, where new social and economic oppression had arisen. They came from Greece, where widespread poverty made it less favorable for Armenians to remain there.

In recent years, the pattern of the dispersion of Armenians is changing again. South America, Australia, and Canada are the principal areas, in addition to the United States, where Armenians are going in their current migrations. These newcomers are a product of relatively modern economies in the countries from which they came. The level of industrialization is higher in most countries they are leaving than it had been in their original homeland in Turkey. Because of this, the newcomers are adapting more easily to their new homes than the earlier immigrants ever could.

PART III

The Armenians in America Today

1. *Population Distribution*

Largely as a result of the early pattern of settlement in the United States, Armenians today live in several distinctly defined areas. This fact can be confirmed in several ways. One good indicator of Armenian population distribution is the number of Armenian churches: the membership rolls and the mailing lists of these churches provides a rough count of people. A second source is the number and kinds of Armenian organizations in America. A third source can be found in the directories of Armenians prepared by individuals or organizations in some areas. Such directories have been compiled simply by going through telephone books or local directories looking for Armenian names. To anyone familiar with them, Armenian names have a characteristic appearance: nearly all of them end in "-ian."

The "-ian" ending of an Armenian name means "of" or "from." Let's take the name "Aram Kevorkian," for example. The family name "Kevorkian" is a surname that means "of Kevork," the Armenian form of the name "George." In the old days, an individual in a community was known by his given name ("Aram," for example). But since there were probably several "Arams" in the community, he was further identified as the Aram of George's family. He then would be called "Aram Kevorkian." Later, when Aram had his own family, his children would be called "Aramian." In more modern times, that practice has been discontinued. Now the family name remains fixed from generation to generation.

Surnames arose not only from given names, but also from some other way that the father was known, such as his trade or some peculiar physical characteristic. If a person was of the baker's family, he would be called "Hatsakordzian." Or if the head of the household happened to be very tall, his children would be called by the name "Yerganian," meaning "of the tall one."

Because of the distinctiveness of Armenian names, it is not too difficult for experts to locate people of Armenian ancestry within the population of the United States. The following table, which was drawn from many sources, gives a fairly reliable estimate of where Armenians live and how numerous they are.

Distribution of Armenians in North America (1970)

The New England States (especially eastern Massachusetts, Rhode Island, Connecticut, and southern New Hampshire)	90,000
The Middle Atlantic States (especially New York City, northern and eastern New York State, northern New Jersey, eastern Pennsylvania, Washington, D.C., and Richmond, Virginia)	175,000
The Southeast (especially the greater Miami area)	15,000
The Middle West (especially the greater Detroit area, Grand Rapids, Chicago, eastern Wisconsin, and St. Louis)	65,000
Central California (especially Fresno and the San Joaquin Valley, the San Francisco Bay Area, and Sacramento)	50,000
Southern California (especially the greater Los Angeles area)	65,000
Elsewhere in the United States	40,000
United States Total:	500,000
Canada (especially Montreal and Toronto)	40,000
Central America (especially Mexico City)	5,000
North American Total:	545,000

2. Occupations

The Armenian community in America is already old enough to have produced two generations of American-born and American-educated Armenians. These people have taken up many occupations and professions. Though their individual talents are based on the heritage they have received from their ancestors, their achievements were made possible by the magnificent educational opportunities they have had in America. Armenians have, of course, entered nearly all fields of endeavor. They have excelled in some, and they have nearly ignored others. Many have entered the fields that call for highly specialized education, such as the learned professions. Even more have followed the tradition of their people and have entered the crafts and trades, becoming metalworkers, machinists, toolmakers, carpenters, shoemakers, tailors, and merchandisers. Very few Armenians have become manual laborers.

Agriculture

When Hagop Seropian left Massachusetts for Fresno in 1881, he found a climate much like that of his native land. His enthusiasm quickly led to the coming of many more Armenians, who settled up and down California's San Joaquin Valley, where Fresno is located. The Armenian community grew with the developing agricultural economy, and today Fresno County has the highest dollar volume of agricultural produce in the entire United States. Many of the Armenian families of Fresno developed new and different agricultural products. The Markarian family showed how figs (both fresh and dried) could be produced and marketed profitably. The Seropians (the first Armenian residents of Fresno) pioneered in the packaging and shipping of dried fruits; today many Armenians are still involved in the fruit-packing business. The Arakelian family imported several types of Armenian melons that grew well in California. Armenians also brought to Fresno new varieties of grapes. The Setrakian family contributed much to

The Seropian Brothers Packing House in 1897. The workers are packing boxes of figs.

the large-scale marketing of raisins, and Armenians have been among the leaders in the production of California wines. Other Armenians planted and operated large-scale farms in vegetables, fruits, and nuts.

When the economic depression struck in 1929, small farms in the Fresno area became unprofitable. Many farmers, including Armenians, lost their heavily mortgaged family farms, which were often bought up and consolidated into larger, more efficient farms. Thus deprived of a livelihood, these farmers would have been a serious economic burden on the community had they remained in Fresno. But most Armenians were not farmers by training; they had their own skills in the trades and crafts. Thus, when they lost their farms, they simply moved to the most promising metropolitan area nearby: Los Angeles. This ability of the Armenians to find other work for themselves and allow an efficient consolidation of farms gave Fresno an important economic advantage. In addition, the movement of Armenians to Los Angeles established what is today a very large Armenian community there.

The Arts

Armenians love nature; they love things that are beautiful in proportion and color, and that are fine in texture and detail. Thus, it is not surprising that several Americans of Armenian ancestry have achieved fame as artists. In the 1920s and 1930s, Hovsep Pushman of Chicago produced lovely still-life paintings with an oriental flavor; his works are now highly prized. Another Armenian artist, Vosdanig Adoian, painted under the name of Arshile Gorky. He was relatively unknown until shortly after his death in 1948, when he suddenly skyrocketed into national prominence. Born in Armenia in 1905, Gorky came to the United States in 1920, after suffering through the Turkish massacres in his homeland. Gorky's art was always haunted by memories of his experiences in Armenia. His well-known painting entitled *The Artist and His Mother* is drawn from these experiences. Based on an old photograph, the picture shows Gorky as a young boy standing beside his sad-eyed mother. The artist's mother died of starvation in Soviet Armenia after the family had fled from Turkey. Gorky himself took his own life when he was only 43 years old.

There are other Armenian-American artists who are still at work today. Khoren Der Harootian of New York creates sculpture of tremendous vitality. His woods, bronzes, and stones portray humanity in its joy and anguish, in life and death. Manuel Tolegian paints still life scenes of rare beauty.

In the field of book illustration, artist Nonny Hogrogian has achieved an enviable reputation. She has twice won the Caldecott

Arshile Gorky's *The Artist and His Mother.* (1926-29. Oil on canvas. 60 x 50 inches. Collection of Whitney Museum of American Art. Gift of Julien Levy for Maro and Natsha Gorky in memory of their father.)

Khoren Der Harootian standing beside his bronze sculpture *Fighting Cocks*

53

Medal awarded by the American Library Association for outstanding picture storybooks for children. *One Fine Day,* the second of Ms. Hogrogian's prize-winning books, tells a story that was inspired by an Armenian folk-tale about the adventures of a greedy fox. The book was both written and illustrated by the artist. Nonny Hogrogian is married to the poet David Kherdian, who is also of Armenian ancestry.

Nonny Hogrogian

Commerce and Finance

The activity of Armenians in the business world has been mostly in exporting and importing. A few Armenians, however, have made notable contributions to domestic commerce. Stephen Mugar of Boston, the founder and owner of Star Markets (now merged with the Jewel Tea Company), is a large merchandiser who has made important innovations in food retailing in supermarkets. His success has been matched by his generous contributions to educational institutions. The late Calouste Gulbenkian, an internationally famous oil magnate, was known as "Mr. Five Percenter." It was through his early recognition of the economic importance of oil that he became the single most important individual in the development of international oil reserves. George Mardikian, owner of the Omar Khayyam restaurant in San Francisco, is a famous restauranteur who volunteered to help the U.S. Armed Forces improve the quality of their food preparation in military installations throughout the world. Kirk Kerkorian, who began as the operator of a charter airline, has built a giant financial empire that controls such huge corporations as Western Airlines and MGM Studios. Finally, in almost every large city in America you will find one or more Armenians in the oriental rug business. One name that has become nationally prominent in the manufacture of domestic carpets is Karagheusian.

George Mardikian

Armen Sarafian

Gregory Adamian

Education

For centuries, Armenians living under the despotic rule of the Ottoman Sultans were denied an opportunity for education. Perhaps it is for that reason that they value education so highly. When the Armenians came to America, they were quick to take advantage of the educational opportunities in this country. As a result, many Armenian men and women have sought careers in education and have become teachers, principals, supervisors, and college professors. In proportion to their numbers, more Armenians have probably found careers in education than in any other field. Some of the more illustrious names must not be overlooked. Sirarpie Der Nersessian is Byzantine Professor Emeritus of Harvard, Wellesley, and Dumbarton Oaks. The cultural heritage of Armenians is a specialty of hers. Three college presidents are Armen Sarafian of La Verne College in California, Barkev Kibarian of Southeastern University in Washington, D.C., and Gregory Adamian of Bentley College in Massachusetts. Zohrab Kaprielian is vice president of the University of Southern California.

Industry and Technology

Several individuals of Armenian descent have built large industrial organizations that are important to the world of American business. Among them are Alex Manoogian of the Masco Corporation in Detroit (manufacturing), Sarkes Tarzian of Sarkes Tarzian, Inc., in Bloomington, Indiana (electronics), Edward Mardigian of the Mardigian Corporation in Detroit (manufacturing), Leon Peters of the Valley Foundry in Fresno (equipment for wine-producing), the four Hovnanian brothers of several New Jersey building and construction firms, and Harry Kuljian of the Kuljian Corporation in Philadelphia (international designers and builders of chemical and industrial processing plants). The Kazanjian family of the Peter-Paul company are the people responsible for the production of candies such as Mounds and Almond Joy. All of these industrial leaders have shared their financial success with the community in philanthropic activities.

Alex Manoogian

Sarkes Tarzian

The original plant of Peter-Paul, Inc., established by the **Kazanjian** family in 1919

You have probably never heard of the Zildjian family of Quincy, Massachusetts, and yet they are world famous. Their cymbals are considered the finest made anywhere. The family name, which they have had for centuries, means "makers of cymbals."

The Law

Many Armenian-Americans have entered the profession of law, but perhaps the most prominent among them is Charles Garry of San Francisco. He has frequently attracted national attention by providing legal counsel for groups active in social struggles. He has also defended such controversial clients as Huey Newton, Bobby Seale, and Angela Davis. Born in 1909 to a poor immigrant family, Garry grew up in a small town in California's San Joaquin Valley. During the 1930s, he attended San Francisco Law School at night, working during the day in his own cleaning and tailoring shop. After receiving his law degree in 1938, Garry embarked on a

Charles Garry

career that would eventually make him one of the nation's best known lawyers.

Journalism and Literature

Several well-known American journalists are proud to claim an Armenian heritage. The newspaper columnist Ben Bagdikian, formerly of Providence, Rhode Island, has attracted national attention for his courageous and crusading reporting. After a career that included managing war news for the U.S. Information Agency, Barry Zorthian became president of Time-Life Cable Communications. Roger Tatarian, formerly Vice President of United Press International, is now Professor of Journalism at California State University, Fresno.

In the field of literature, two writers named Arlen—a father and son—have made names for themselves in very different ways. Their story had its beginnings in the year 1892, when a family named Kouyoumdjian fled Armenia to escape persecution by the Turks. They traveled first to Bulgaria, where Mrs. Kouyoumdjian gave birth to a son, Dikran. The Kouyoumdjians eventually settled in England, and Dikran was educated there. In his early 20s, he went to London, where he became friends with the artists and writers of the period, among them the famous British novelist D. H. Lawrence. Within 10 years, Dikran Kouyoumdjian had published two collections of short stories and two novels, all under the pen name of "Michael Arlen," which he later took as his legal name. His second novel, *The Green Hat,* was a smashing success both as a book and, later, as a play. Its subject was the sophisticated world of British high society, which Arlen had come to know very well.

Although Michael Arlen was known primarily as a British writer, he worked more and more in the United States as time went on. Eventually he wrote screenplays in Hollywood and supervised the production of his plays both on the east and the west coasts. Arlen moved to America during World War II, and he spent the last 15 years of his life living and working in this country. He died in 1956.

Michael Arlen's son, Michael J. Arlen, is now a successful professional writer in the United States. He has published many short stories, articles, and reviews, but his two most recent books, *Exiles* (1970) and *Passage to Ararat* (1975), are perhaps the most interesting part of his work. *Exiles* is the story of his father, the senior Michael Arlen, cut off from his Armenian homeland and seeking a new life in the English-speaking world. *Passage to Ararat* describes the younger Arlen's personal search for his Armenian roots. This book was honored by the literary world in 1976, when it received a National Book Award in the category of Contemporary Affairs.

The most famous Armenian-American in the literary world is undoubtedly William Saroyan, a novelist, playwright, screen

Michael J. Arlen   **William Saroyan**

writer, and film director. Born in Fresno in 1908, Saroyan began his literary career by writing short stories. He established himself as a leading American writer when he published a collection of stories in 1934 entitled *The Daring Young Man on the Flying Trapeze.* Saroyan most often writes about simple people and touching human situations; many of his works depict the lives of the Armenians in Europe and America. He has now published more than 30 books and plays in the course of his career. Saroyan has won both the Pulitzer Prize and the New York Drama Critics' Circle Award, two of the most esteemed honors that the literary world can bestow.

Medical Science

Thousands of Armenians have entered the fields of medicine and dentistry in America, and they have attained success at all levels of achievement, from general practice to advanced specialization. There are many outstanding professionals in the field of medicine, but we shall mention only two of them here.

Dr. John S. Najarian

Dr. Varaztad H. Kazanjian, Professor Emeritus of Plastic Surgery at Harvard University, was one of the founders of this new and amazing science. He long held a unique position for his immense knowledge and skill, and he was regularly sought after for consultation. His methods of corrective and restorative plastic surgery on the face and the exposed parts of the body have brought new hope to people whose lives might otherwise have been ruined by deformity and disfigurement.

Dr. John S. Najarian, Chairman of the Department of Surgery at the University of Minnesota Medical School, is a world-famous transplant surgeon. He was born in California in 1927 and, after receiving his medical education there, joined the faculty of the University of California Medical School, where he worked until moving to Minnesota in 1967. His pioneering work in kidney transplant surgery has literally given new life to hundreds of kidney disease victims, saving them from a long and painful period of gradual deterioration and almost certain death.

Music

In writing his *St. Vardan* Symphony, composer Alan Hovhaness reached deep into his Armenian heritage and gave it modern musical expression. This important figure in modern music was born in Massachusetts in 1911, the child of an Armenian father and a Scottish mother. He studied at the New England Conservatory, and became interested in Armenian music at the age of 30, by which time he had become an accomplished pianist and composer. Hovhaness' interest in Armenian music led him to explore the entire world of Oriental music, and he became fascinated with the complex musical themes and rhythms of India, Korea, and other eastern countries. Eventually, he began to incorporate these eastern musical ideas into his own compositions, blending them with the western musical traditions of his earlier formal training.

Hovhaness has produced an immense body of music in his lifetime. He is especially fond of curious and unusual combinations

Alan Hovhaness

Lucine Amara as Pamina in *The Magic Flute*

of instruments: his Symphony No. 16 is written for strings and Korean percussion, and another composition calls only for tympani, drums, tamtam, marimba, and glockenspiel!

Other Americans of Armenian ancestry have also made contributions in the world of music. Richard Yardumian has been much in demand as a composer of orchestral pieces and other special works. The sopranos Lucine Amara and Lili Chookasian are members of the Metropolitan Opera Company, and mezzo-soprano Edna Garabedian was a winner at the Moscow Tchaikowsky competition in 1970. The rising young tenor Vahan Khanzadian may someday match the fame of the former Metropolitan tenor Armand Tokatyan. Bassos Ara Berberian and Michael Kermoyan are making their names in opera and in musicals, and the versatile soprano Cathy Berberian has brought an unusual dimension to the use of the voice in her daring performances.

From a very early age, the brilliant Ajemian sisters gave the musical world fine piano and violin performances. In the field of violin teaching, no name is more prominent than that of Ivan

Galamian of the Curtis Institute of Music. And two brothers named Kojian appear prominently in American symphonic orchestras, one as conductor and the other as concert master.

Public Service

Although Armenians have not entered politics or sought public office on a large scale, a few names do stand out in public service. In the executive branch of the government, Paul R. Ignatius held the position of Secretary of the Navy from 1967 to 1969. Robert Mardian served in the Justice Department during the Nixon administration. Two Armenian-Americans have held seats in the United States House of Representatives: Steven Derounian of New York served from 1963 to 1964, and Adam Benjamin, Jr., whose mother is Armenian, was elected in 1976 to represent the state of Indiana. Several Armenians have served in state legislatures, including George Deukmejian, a member of the California State Senate, Walter Karabian, a member of the California State Assembly, and Harout Sanasarian, a member of the Wisconsin House of Representatives.

Science

Armenians are very strongly represented throughout America's scientific and technical institutions, research organizations, and universities. They are especially prominent in the fields of mathematics, physics, chemistry, and the modern descendents of these fields—computer sciences, nuclear physics and biochemistry. Dr. G. K. Daghlian was a mathematician and physicist who sacrificed his life in America's atomic energy research. Vazken Parsegian of the Rensselaer Institute has written a number of highly regarded physics texts. Armig Kandoian was, until recently, Director of the U.S. Office of Telecommunications. Emik Avakian, though greatly disabled by cerebral palsy, has made many valuable contributions in the field of computer systems.

Ara Parseghian

Sports

Perhaps the most outstanding Armenian name in the world of sports is that of Ara Parseghian, one of the most successful football coaches in history. After brilliant coaching records at Miami of Ohio and at Northwestern, Parseghian was named head coach of the legendary Notre Dame football team in 1963. In 11 years at Notre Dame, his teams won 94 games and finished among the top 10 college football teams during each of those 11 consecutive years. In 1974, Parseghian resigned from this illustrious job to relax and spend more time with his family.

Entertainment

A number of Armenians have been prominent in the entertainment world. In television, there have been Arlene Frances (Kazanjian), Cher (Sarkisian) of Sonny and Cher, David Hedison, and Kay Armen (Manoogian). Rouben Mamoulian, who directed the motion pictures *Oklahoma* and *Porgy and Bess,* is known as one of the finest directors in the entertainment world. Akim Tamirof played character roles in the movies, and Leon Danielian has been the director of the American Ballet Theater.

One of the best known performers of Armenian ancestry is Mike Connors, who played Joe Mannix in the "Mannix" television series for many years. Born Krekor Ohanian in Fresno, Connors became a basketball star while attending college at UCLA. Although he was planning to pursue a career as a lawyer, Hollywood talent scouts convinced him to study acting. Working his way up from the bottom, Connors even took a job as a door-to-door salesman until he could support himself and his young family by acting. His television show had the longest run of any private detective series, and it remained at the top of the ratings year after year.

Rouben Mamoulian

Mike Connors

3. Religious, Social, and Cultural Life

The Church

The church is still the focus of Armenian community life. Although not all Armenians attend church regularly, many of them participate in the community activities associated with the church, such as weddings, baptisms, funerals, and holiday services. Most Armenians belong to the mother, or national, church, which became independent at the beginning of the sixth century. But during the 19th century, two different groups of Armenians formed other Armenian churches. One group joined the worldwide Roman Catholic community and now recognizes the Pope as their spiritual head. We shall call them "Armenian Catholics," though they are sometimes also called "Uniats." Their ritual, called the "eastern rite," is virtually identical to that used in the Armenian Church. The second group organized churches that belong to one or another of the Protestant denominations. These churches are mainly Evangelical and have ties with the Congregationalists and the Presbyterians. Their services are similar to those of other Protestant churches, although much of the ritual is conducted in the modern Armenian language. Other parts of the service are conducted in English (or in the language of the country in which the church is located).

There are 89 national Armenian churches in existence at this time, located in various regions of the United States and Canada.

Armenian Church Communities in the United States & Canada (1976)

New England	18
Middle Atlantic	25
Midwest	17
California	21
Elsewhere in the U.S.	3
Canada	5
Total	89

Vazgen I, spiritual head of the Armenian Church

These church organizations are officially divided between two dioceses, the eastern and the western. The western diocese covers California, and the eastern diocese covers the rest of the United States, plus Canada. At the head of each diocese is a bishop. The priesthood is divided into two classes: the married class and the celibate, or unmarried, class. Although the Armenian Church permits parish priests to marry, only the celibate priests may rise in the church hierarchy to become bishops.

The world political situation has created some serious problems in the administration of the many far-flung dioceses of the Armenian Church throughout the world. The spiritual head of the church resides in Etjmiatzin, in the Armenian Soviet Socialist Republic—part of the U.S.S.R. Since the communist government there does not support organized religion, it is difficult for the head of the church to provide spiritual and administrative leadership for the many dioceses throughout the world. Because of this problem, there are some groups of Armenians who feel that Armenia should be a free and independent nation rather than a part of the Soviet Union. Their unhappiness with the political situation in Soviet Armenia has led them to form a separately administered church organization, with a separate spiritual leader, who resides in Antelias, Lebanon. This organization has also established dioceses in the United States. As a result, there are now two rival sets of dioceses existing side by side, each set owing allegiance to a different spiritual leader. Representatives of both groups are now seeking to remove the barriers between them, so that there will eventually be only one diocese in each geographical area.

Another problem that the church is trying to solve is the shortage of American-born clergymen. Few American-born Armenians have been interested in a career in the service of the church. As a result, most members of the clergy have been brought in from countries where Armenians are more numerous and where the young people have full command of the Armenian language. But now the American dioceses have established the St. Nersess Theological Seminary in New York to give American-born young men an opportunity to become clergymen in the mother church.

The Armenian Catholic and Protestant communities are much smaller than the communities of the mother church. But because Armenian Catholics and Protestants belong to these groups by choice (rather than simply by tradition), they often have a better record of church attendance. There are 4 Armenian Catholic and 26 Armenian Protestant churches in the United States and Canada. The Protestant churches are joined together in two larger organizations, the Armenian Missionary Association of America and the Armenian Evangelical Union of North America.

All of the churches have associated with them a number of auxiliary or affiliated organizations, such as men's clubs, couples' clubs, youth groups, ladies' auxiliaries, and so on. There are Sunday schools for religious education, in which the Armenian traditions and beliefs are taught in English. Some of the churches also conduct classes for the teaching of such subjects as the Armenian language, Armenian history, and Armenian culture.

Social, Charitable, and Cultural Organizations

Organizations and their activities are a very important part of life for Armenians in America. Though the Armenian organizations may be primarily social, charitable, cultural, or even political, most of them combine all of these characteristics in varying degrees. Some are worldwide in scope, with branches or chapters in this country. Others are only national or even local, but they may be equally influential.

The Armenian General Benevolent Union is primarily a charitable organization first founded 70 years ago to help needy Armenians in the Near East. Today it serves the needs of Armenians all over the world, and it operates schools in the Near East and in America. The Armenian Relief Society, primarily a women's organization, serves in essentially the same manner. The Knights of Vartan are members of a fraternal organization dedicated to the moral and cultural uplift of its members and of the community. The Armenian Students' Association of America attempts to create a favorable environment for students in colleges and universities by providing scholarship aid, by bringing them together in social events, and by creating an awareness of the Armenian heritage. The Armenian Assembly, a newly established group of Armenian community leaders from all over America, seeks to foster cooperation among the various other organizations, so as to fill the needs of the whole community. These organizations are national in scope, having branches or chapters in many cities.

Armenians feel a strong loyalty to the particular Old World city from which they or their ancestors originally came. As a result,

Participants at a national conference of the Armenian Youth Federation discuss the history and the role of the Armenian woman. Held in Rock Creek, Ohio, in 1977, the conference was attended by young Armenian-Americans from all over the United States.

there are several patriotic organizations that bind together those who have connections with the same Old World community. These organizations also do charitable work, and they serve to instill in the newer generations an awareness of their heritage.

In communities where Armenians are numerous, there are often organizations that provide modern homes for the aged. Other organizations promote athletics. They periodically hold athletic meets, where they form teams for competition in such sports as basketball and soccer.

In the period when Armenians were struggling to gain their independence and to preserve their existence as a nation, a number of Armenian political organizations were formed to promote the welfare of the Armenian people as a whole. These organizations still exist today, working within the framework of the governments or nations under which they exist. They continue to carry on work that promotes within the Armenian community an understanding of the basic political problem that faces Armenians. Within the framework of these political organizations are a number of affiliated groups, such as youth groups. These supplement the work of the parent organizations and provide training and experience for those who will one day become leaders themselves. Perhaps the most important activity of these political organizations is that of publishing Armenian-language newspapers There are several newspapers in circulation at this time, ranging from dailies to weeklies.

In addition to the newspapers printed in Armenian, there are several English-language weeklies: the *Armenian Mirror-Spectator,* the *Armenian Weekly,* the *Armenian Reporter,* the *California Courier,* and the *Armenian Observer.* Other periodicals published in both Armenian and English are *The Armenian Review, Ararat,* and *The Armenian Church,* as well as the publications of some of the larger political organizations.

There are also in existence nonpolitical groups that stress the academic and cultural aspects of community life. Some cultural groups, such as the Tekeyan Cultural Association, the Armenian Cultural Association, and the Armenian Literary Society (as well as various dramatic, choral, and dance groups), stress Armenian culture itself. But other groups, such as the Armenian Allied Arts Association and the Armenian Professional Society, are formed of Armenians who share a common cultural or intellectual interest that is itself not necessarily Armenian in nature.

The National Association for Armenian Studies and Research promotes Armenian scholarship in institutions of higher learning. It was primarily responsible for the establishment of chairs of Armenian studies at Harvard University, the University of California at Los Angeles, and Columbia University. Serious work in Armenian studies is also carried on at the University of Pennsylvania, California State University at Fresno, Wayne State University, and the University of Massachusetts. More limited programs in Armenian studies are offered at about 25 other institutions.

In several cities in Massachusetts, public schools offer limited courses at the high-school level, primarily in the Armenian language. In 1965, a movement was started to establish full-time Armenian day schools. These schools provide for full primary and secondary education, fulfulling all public school requirements and, in addition, providing education in the language, history, and culture of the Armenian people. There are now 12 full-time Armenian day schools, and their work has been crowned with success. They are found in the Los Angeles area, in Philadelphia, Detroit, Boston, and Montreal. More such schools are being planned in other cities.

4. *Integration into American Life*

The earliest Armenians came to America as isolated individuals. They were few in number and had little opportunity to mix with other Armenians. In general, they lived alone, often as students, and they sometimes made friends with other students, families, and social groups without ever meeting any other Armenians. When Armenians began to arrive as refugees and as families in 1890, however, they naturally remained in closely knit groups. The New World, though as friendly as could be expected, was still a strange place. They knew neither its language nor its customs. Moreover, the immigrants had little material wealth. For the most part, they had only what they could earn in wages. Yet many sent money back to the Old World to help the other members of their families who had remained behind. Others saved their earnings, hoping to return to their homeland if conditions improved there. Still others saved to procure passage for other members of the families to come to America. Thus, it was common for these people to stick together and to live as economically as possible.

Until the 1920s, Armenians generally lived close together and formed ghetto-like areas inside the American cities they inhabited.

After World War I, however, it became evident to the Armenians in America that their future was in this country, not in the Old World. Only then did they begin to think about integrating themselves into American life more completely. Thus, beginning in 1920, Armenians began to plan for their futures as part of the over-all pattern of American life. They began to move out of their ghettoes and disperse into the communities where they lived. They were able to make such moves because by that time their economic position had improved sufficiently to permit it.

During the 1920s, Armenians living in large numbers in American communities began to experience discrimination from their non-Armenian neighbors. This was especially true in Fresno, where Armenians made up over 10 percent of the total population. Their presence in the community was resented by the rest of the population, which often did not understand traditional Armenian habits and manners. As a result of this resentment and misunderstanding, the Armenians became the object of irrational prejudices and felt the pain of discrimination. In many areas of the city, they were not even permitted to buy property. Their children grew up in a tense environment, unable to understand why they should tolerate the prejudice and disrespect with which they were being treated.

In time, the air in Fresno cleared. The economic depression of the 1930s and the experience of World War II broadened people's understanding. Discriminatory laws and practices that had been used against Armenians were eventually struck down as illegal. And, most important, the Armenians themselves bore up under the malice shown toward them. By their own efforts, they improved their situation in all ways. Today Armenians live in Fresno and other cities as a very natural part of the community, blending with it and yet not sacrificing their rich cultural heritage. They participate fully in the life of the community and, at the same time, enrich it by sharing their own heritage.

This statue of the legendary Armenian hero David of Sassoon was erected in Fresno, California, in honor of the contributions of Armenians to the city's history.

One result of the increased integration of Armenians into American life has been intermarriage. As is the case with most Americans these days, large numbers of Armenians are marrying outside their ethnic group. There are no accurate statistics available, but it has been estimated that as many as half of the marriages involving Armenians are mixed. When these marriages occur, however, the wedding ceremony is still likely to take place in an Armenian church, or in a non-Armenian church with an Armenian clergyman officiating. Civil marriages are still rare among Armenians.

For the Armenian people, intermarriage is a new experience. Living for many years as members of closely knit communities with strong religious and cultural ties, Armenians have traditionally found marriage partners among their own people. But as Armenian life in the United States has changed and expanded, attitudes toward mixed marriages have changed too, becoming more tolerant and relaxed. These new attitudes are another indication of Armenian assimilation into American society.

At present, there are some Armenians who think there has been too much assimilation, as well as others who think there is still not enough. The process of Armenian integration into American life has gone through its early phases, when the changes were dramatic and easily observed. Now the situation has reached a kind of steady state. Time will tell whether the Armenian community in America will manage to maintain its identity as an ethnic group, preserving all that is best of its own heritage and sharing that heritage with the nation as a whole. The leaders of the Armenian community are passionately interested in this question, and it is frequently the main topic of discussion in gatherings and formal meetings of Armenian-Americans today.

PART IV

What Does the Future Hold?

1. *Language*

Most young Armenians in America today no longer speak Armenian. This is not surprising. Their parents belonged to a generation that was concerned with becoming economically successful, obtaining the best education, and adapting to the American way of life. This generation largely ignored its cultural heritage, and therefore its children did not learn Armenian. But there are three exceptions to this overall picture. A few families, even in the third generation, managed to keep alive the tradition of speaking Armenian in the home. Their children did learn to speak and understand Armenian to some extent. The second exception is due to the continual flow of new Armenian immigrants into the United States from countries such as Turkey, Lebanon, Syria, and Persia. In these countries, the Armenian community is stronger, there are Armenian schools, and the language is used for everyday communication.

The third exception stems from the reawakening of interest in the Armenian language that has developed within recent years among Armenian-Americans. This interest has given rise to the opening of Armenian day schools in many cities. Such private schools are faced with a challenge. They must offer the full curriculum of subjects that are taught in the public schools and, *in addition*, teach Armenian language, history, and culture. These additions lengthen the school day, but neither parents nor pupils

A class at the Alex Manoogian School in Southfield, Michigan. This private Armenian day school is run by the Armenian General Benevolent Union.

appear to mind. These schools seem to be more successful in educating the children than the public schools, even in general subjects, perhaps because the students who attend them are more strongly motivated.

We can only guess what the future holds for the use of the Armenian language in the United States. In the foreseeable future, more private Armenian day schools will probably be opened, where pupils will learn to speak and read Armenian. But it is also likely that the number of such schools will never contain more than a small percentage of Armenian children. Our guess is that the total number of pupils in all private Armenian day schools throughout America will level off at 10,000, about 10 percent of all school-age children. But this is purely a guess. We also think that Armenian study programs at institutions of higher learning will continue to grow and to attract more and more students.

2. *The Church*

The Armenian Church is struggling to satisfy two very different needs. One is to preserve the age-old religious traditions that have survived through so many crises. The other is to respond to the changing needs of modern society, especially in America. The religious traditions of the mother church involve elaborate rituals and services based on complex philosophical ideas. The language used is the classical language, which is understood only by a few. Today, many talk of converting the services to modern Armenian, and some even speak of using English. Even if that were done, however, those attending church would probably still find it difficult to understand the true meaning of the liturgies.

Only a small percentage of the total Armenian population attends the mother church. In a typical city where there is a large Armenian population, there will probably be one church for each 3,000 to 4,000 Armenians, including the Catholic and Protestant Armenian churches. But average attendance on regular Sundays may be only 150 to 200 people. (Of course, many of the remaining Armenians attend other, non-Armenian, churches.) On special feast days, however, attendance at Armenian churches is much higher. Why do so few Armenians attend the mother church regularly? The answer lies in a number of factors: the problem of understanding the classical language, the scattered settlement of Armenians today, and the fact that the American environment does not seem to encourage worship in the ancient way, even though the rituals are beautiful to see and to hear. Another reason for this lack of interest is that the protection and guidance provided by the church in the homeland is no longer needed in America.

Nevertheless, the mother church seems to be holding its own for the time being, despite these problems. Although not very many young people attend church, there still seem to be enough of them to keep the church going. Armenians still love their church and want it to be strong. Despite its uncertain future, they are constantly replacing the older church buildings with new, more beautiful, and more expensive ones. Moreover, these new churches are being built in the tradition of ancient Armenian church architecture, where contemporary architectural features are blended in with the classical ones. And the new churches include facilities for other activities. There are classrooms for the church Sunday school, gymnasiums for athletic activities, meeting rooms for young people's groups, and large halls for meetings of the church community.

3. Assimilation

A generation ago, many members of the Armenian community, observing the changes in the living habits of the Armenian families they knew, would shake their heads and say sorrowfully that in 50 years the Armenian community would no longer exist. "The Armenian community will dissolve into the American mainstream," they would say. "Soon, there will no longer be any Armenian-Americans left." But that has not happened. Today the Armenian community is vigorous. This is not to say that it resembles the Armenian community of 50 years ago; the community is strong in a different way. It has lived through a period of adjustment. It has modified its way of life, blending elements from its own rich heritage with elements from the culture of the American mainstream. In the minds of most people, this is a happy blend. Armenians believe that they have preserved what was important in their cultural heritage while, at the same time, embracing the fullness of American life. Finally, the preservation of the Armenian community in America has been made more secure by the small

The cultural heritage of the past is important to most modern Armenian-Americans.

but continual flow of immigrants from the more traditional Armenian societies of the Middle East. Their entrance into the community provides a kind of leavening or sweetening. They too help keep the Armenian-American community vigorous.

Thus, the Armenian community in America is now in a stable situation. It has lived through the difficulties of social and economic adjustment. It has emerged with a satisfactory blend of its own cultural heritage with the American environment. It has retained a reasonable level of vigor in its basic institutions: the church and the Armenian language. The Armenian community in America is not about to disappear, and it is fortunate for America that this is so. As long as the Armenian community is strong and well, it can continue to add its own special contribution to the rich tapestry of cultures that has always made this country unique among the nations of the world.

... INDEX ...

Daghlian, Dr. G. K., 65
Danielian, Leon, 67
Der Harootian, Khoren, 52
Der Nersessian, Sirapie, 56
Derounian, Steven, 65
Deukmejian, George, 65
discrimination against Armenian-
    Americans, 75-76

education in traditional Armenian
    society, 29-31, 56
Etjmiatzin (Soviet Union), 69

family in traditional Armenian
    society, 26-27
Frances, Arlene, 66
Fresno, California, Armenian
    community in, 41, 50, 51-52,
    75-76

Galamian, Ivan, 64-65
Garabedian, Edna, 64
Garry, Charles, 58-59
"George the Armenian," 38
Gorky, Arshile, 52
grabar (written form of Armenian
    language), 17
Gregory, Saint, 14
Gulbenkian, Calouste, 54-55

Hai, 12
Haiastan, 12
Haik, 12
Hedison, David, 66
Hogrogian, Nonny, 52, 54
Hovhaness, Alan, 41-42
Hovnanian brothers, 57

Ignatius, Paul R., 65
illuminated manuscripts, Armenian,
17

immigration, restriction of, in 1924,
    45-46
intermarriage among Armenian-
    Americans, 76-77

Jamestown, 38

Kandoian, Armig, 65
Kaprielian, Zohrab, 56
Karabian, Walter, 65
Karagheusian (carpet manufacturers),
    55
Kazanjian family, 57
Kazanjian, Dr. Varaztad H., 62
Kerkorian, Kirk, 55
Kermoyan, Michael, 64
Khanzadian, Vakan, 64
Kherdian, David, 54
Kibarian, Barkev, 56

language, Armenian, 7, 16-17, 19,
    78-79, 80, 82
Leon V (last Armenian king), 21

Mamoulian, Rouben, 66-67
Manoogian, Alex, 57
Mardian, Robert, 65
Mardigian, Edward, 57
Mardikian, George, 55
Markarian family, 50
marriage in traditional Armenian
    society, 27-28
"Martin the Armenian," 38
massacres of Armenians by Turks,
    8, 22-23, 42
Mesrop (Armenian scholar), 16
Movses of Khoren, 12
Mugar, Stephen, 54

Najarian, Dr. John S., 62
National Association for Armenian
    Studies and Research, 73

occupations of Armenian-
  Americans, 50
organizations, Armenian, 71-73
Oskanian, Khachik, 38, 39-40
Ottoman Turks, 21, 39

Parseghian, Ara, 66
Parsegian, Vazken, 65
Persia, 14
population distribution of
  Armenians: in 19th century, 35;
  in early 20th century, 36; in
  recent times, 8-9, 36-37, 47, 48-49
Pushman, Hovsep, 32

religion, Armenian, 13-16
Rome, 20, 21
Russia, 24-25

Sahak (patriarch), 16
Saint Nersess Theological
  Seminary, 70
Sanasarian, Harout, 65
Sarafian, Armen, 56
Saroyan, William, 60-61
Seljuk Turks, 21
Seropian, Hagop, 50
Seropian, Kristapor, 40
Setrakian family, 50-51
Sevan, Lake, 11

silk culture in colonial America, 38

Tamirof, Akim, 67
Tarzian, Sarkes, 57
Tatarian, Roger, 59
Tekeyan Cultural Association, 73
Thaddeus (apostle), 13-14
Theophany, 31
Tigranes II (Armenian king), 19, 20
Tigris-Euphrates Valley, 7
Tiridates (Armenian king), 14
Tokatyan, Armand, 64
Tolegian, Manuel, 52
Turkey, 22-23, 25, 39, 42, 45
Turkish Empire, 33, 39
Turks, 8, 21; massacres of
  Armenians by, 22-23

Uniats, 68
Urartu, 11

Van, Lake, 11

World War I, 22, 24, 45, 46
World War II, 46

Yardumian, Richard, 64

Zildjian family, 58
Zoroastrianism, 14
Zorthian, Barry, 59

ABOUT THE AUTHOR . . .

Arra S. Avakian has been deeply involved in Armenian community life and in the study of Armenian culture for many years. After a distinguished career in the fields of scientific research and engineering, Dr. Avakian was appointed professor of Armenian Studies at California State University, Fresno, in 1970. Six years later, he took a similar position at the newly formed American Armenian International College in La Verne, California. Dr. Avakian has also taught many classes in the Armenian language and has developed a series of television programs dealing with Armenian culture. He has been active in such community organizations as the Armenian Students' Association of America, the National Association for Armenian Studies and Research, and the Armenian Assembly. Among his special interests are the music and the liturgy of the Armenian Church. Dr. Avakian has written a manual on Armenian choral music, in addition to numerous newspaper and magazine articles on other Armenian subjects. He and his family make their home in Fresno, California.

The IN AMERICA *Series*

We specialize in publishing quality books for
young people. For a complete list please write:

LERNER PUBLICATIONS COMPANY
241 First Avenue North, Minneapolis, Minnesota 55401